CONTENTS

Some words are printed in bold, **like this**. You can find out what they mean by looking in the glossary.

THE WILL OF THE PEOPLE

In 2010, citizens across Iraq entered schools and gave their names. Someone checked a list of all the people who had **registered** to vote. People whose names were on the list received a paper **ballot**. This ballot had the names of all the local **candidates** running for Iraq's **parliament**. The voters put their own names on the ballot, then went off by themselves to mark their choices.

All the completed ballots went into large plastic bins, so they could be counted later. Then, the voters dipped one finger in ink. The ink would show everyone that they had voted—which meant they could not legally vote again.[1] Thanks in part to this system, the election of 2010 was the fairest in Iraqi history.[2]

In countries holding their first free elections, such as Iraq, voters often proudly display the ink on their fingers that show they voted.

Voting and Elections

Michael Burgan

Heinemann
LIBRARY
Chicago, Illinois

www.capstonepub.com

Visit our website to find out more information about Heinemann-Raintree books.

To order:

☎ Phone 800-747-4992

🖳 Visit www.capstonepub.com to browse our catalog and order online.

Edited by Adam Miller, Louise Galpine, and Adrian Vigliano
Designed by Marcus Bell
Original illustrations © Capstone Global Library Ltd.
Illustrated by Darren Lingard
Picture research by Tracy Cummins
Production by Alison Parsons
Originated by Capstone Global Library Ltd.
Printed and bound in China by Leo Paper Products Ltd.

16 15 14 13 12
10 9 8 7 6 5 4 3 2 1

Library of Congress Cataloging-in-Publication Data
Burgan, Michael.
  Voting and elections / Michael Burgan.
    p. cm.—(Ethics of politics)
  Includes bibliographical references and index.
  ISBN 978-1-4329-6552-5 (hbk.)—ISBN 978-1-4329-6557-0 (pbk.) 1. Voting—Juvenile literature. 2. Elections—Juvenile literature. I. Title.
  JF1001.B775 2012
  324.6—dc23   2011044115

Acknowledgments
The author and publishers are grateful to the following for permission to reproduce copyright material: Corbis pp. 9 (© Bettmann), 27 (© Haydn West/epa), 37 (© CORBIS), 48 (© LIRIO DA FONSECA/X01340/Reuters); Getty Images pp. 7 (Leemage), 12 (Robert King/Newsmakers), 16 (Jahi Chikwendiu/The Washington Post), 21 (Marty Melville), 23 (FREDERIC J. BROWN/AFP), 28 (Scott Olson), 35 (AFP PHOTO / ALBERTO PIZZOLI), 40 (JOEL SAGET/AFP), 45 (WALEED AHMAD/AFP), 50 (GABRIEL BOUYS/AFP); istockphoto pp. 11 (© jcarillet), 19 (© Chris Schmidt), 25 (© tirc83); Library of Congress Prints and Photographs Division pp. 26, 42; Shutterstock pp. 4 (© homeros), 31 (© Frontpage), 46 (© homeros), 39 (© Robert Park), 53 (© Frontpage).

Cover photograph of a Sudanese voter casting a ballot reproduced with the permission of Getty Images (ROBERTO SCHMIDT/AFP).

We would like to thank Jonathan Lipman for his invaluable help in the preparation of this book.

Every effort has been made to contact copyright holders of any material reproduced in this book. Any omissions will be rectified in subsequent printings if notice is given to the publisher.

"Everyone has the right to take part in the government of his country, directly or through freely chosen representatives."[3]

United Nations Universal Declaration of Human Rights

Democracy in action

As these people discovered, people perform an important function when they vote. Voting and elections are part of the **political** process. *Politics* refers to the system used to construct a government and decide how that government is run.

A government based on the free, fair elections of public officials is called a **representative democracy**. Voters choose people to represent their views. These elected officials then go on to run their country's government and shape its **policies**. People who live in representative democracies believe they have the best form of government in the world. It gives people great freedom to shape their own lives.

But some countries have different systems. Saudi Arabia, for example, is a kingdom. Voters cannot choose national leaders. Cuba, a **communist** country, limits who can run for office.[4] The rulers of these countries value order—or keeping their own power—rather than giving people the greatest freedom possible. Also, all countries that have elections are not necessarily democracies.[5] Rulers sometimes arrange who can run for office and who can vote in such a way that citizens don't have true freedom to choose their elected officials.

The ethics of voting and elections

Given the importance of voting and elections in democracies, people want to ensure that the process is totally fair. But there are many challenges to having open and fair elections. Indeed, voting and elections raise many difficult **ethical** questions. **Ethics** is the study of deciding which kinds of behavior are right and wrong.

For example, sometimes people are influenced to vote a certain way. This raises many ethical questions about fairness. The way that votes are counted is another ethical question. So is the role of money in determining who wins an election. Deciding who can and cannot vote raises more ethical questions, as do many other issues. By looking more closely at the ethics of voting and elections, we can better understand how truly free and fair a **democratic** country is.

5

DEMOCRACY THROUGH THE AGES

The word **democracy** comes from the Greek words *demos*, meaning "people," and *kratos*, meaning "rule." In other words, it means "rule by the people." Rule by the people involves voting and elections. These ideas have roots in ancient history.

Ancient Greece and Rome

In ancient Greece, Athens was the best example of a Greek democracy. Voters did not choose representatives to express their views. Instead, all male citizens met to discuss and vote on how the city should handle its affairs. This kind of democracy is sometimes called a **direct democracy**, meaning citizens are directly involved in making decisions. But Athens and the other Greek cities also had elections. Voters chose military leaders and officials called *archons*, who helped run the cities.

Direct democracy combined with human nature created ethical problems. For example, what if a single person started to become too powerful? In Athens, a special election served to limit the power of anyone who seemed a threat to the city. In a first vote, the citizens answered yes or no to the question: "Is anyone a danger?" If the majority of voters said yes, a second vote was held. Voters wrote the name of the person they feared as a threat on a piece of pottery called an *ostrakon*. The person whose name appeared the most was forced to leave the city for 10 years.[1] The process is known today as ostracism. (The word also applies to excluding or avoiding someone who goes against a group's rules or values.)

Several hundred years after the rise of Athens, Rome began to build one of the largest empires ever. For a time, Rome had elements of direct democracy as well as elections.

The Romans split their government into three distinct branches with their own functions. The **legislative** branch made laws. All voters took part in approving laws. They also elected various officials of the **executive** branch, such as consuls and tribunes. The executives carried out laws. Together, executive officials and juries made up of citizens formed the **judicial** branch. They made sure laws were carried out fairly.[2]

These pieces of pottery were used in ancient Greece almost 2,500 years ago during the voting to ostracize dangerous citizens.

The ancient Greeks and Romans had detailed written laws that explained how their governments ran. Greek citizens watched closely to make sure no one proposed actions that violated existing laws.[3] Laws set the ethical standards by which everyone lived. This idea of the "rule of law" was influential for many later governments (see page 13).

Roots of democracy in Great Britain

While voting goes back thousands of years, many notions of democratic government come from the **constitution** of Great Britain. A constitution lays out laws that can resolve the ethical questions that arise in a government.

The process of creating Britain's constitution began in 1215. Wealthy landowners called barons forced England's King John to share some of his power with them. This arrangement was spelled out in a document called Magna Carta.

In 1254, British counties began to elect representatives to send to Parliament, where they could discuss taxes with the king.[4] Over time, lawmakers argued with the king on various issues, such as taxes and religion. Parliament sometimes thought the king violated the constitution. During the 1640s, the disagreements led to a civil war and the killing of King Charles I.

Fighting for the right to vote in Britain

The British **monarchy** was restored in 1661. Then, in 1688, England had what has been called its Glorious Revolution. It was glorious partly because important change came without bloodshed. But the true glory of this revolution was the rights the new **monarchs**, William and Mary, promised to uphold.

Added to the country's constitution, which was unwritten (see page 13), was the Declaration of Rights. One of those rights was the guarantee of free elections for members of Parliament. In the past, certain kings had tried to influence voting, so that the men they wanted in government would be elected. At times the kings actually threw out the results if they did not like who won. The Declaration of Rights ended the monarchy's unethical election practices.[5] This set an important ethical standard for future democracies.

Another major change came with the Reform Act of 1832. This extended the right to vote. This law also gave new cities more representatives, reflecting their rising populations.[6]

Voting in North America

England's North American colonists had their own concerns about voting and representation. They enjoyed the long English tradition of choosing local leaders and representatives. And through the 17th and most of the 18th centuries, England did not pay much attention to colonial affairs.

But starting in 1764, the British Parliament's need for money led to new taxes on the North American **colonies**. Some colonists opposed the new taxes. Under the English constitution, they believed, only people elected by the voters could call for a tax. Yet the colonists did not have representatives in Parliament. So, some colonists began speaking out against the idea of "taxation without representation." To them, it was unethical to make someone pay a tax if they had no say in shaping it or a chance to speak out against it. This tax issue was one reason why the North American colonists fought their successful war for independence, starting in 1775.

"I think the Parliament of Great Britain hath no more right to put their hand into my pocket, without my consent, than I have to put my hands into yours for money."[7]

George Washington, the first U.S. president

Revolution in France: Creating a real democracy

During this same period, revolution was also brewing in France. Among the issues causing conflict was the idea that all French citizens should express their will through their elected officials.

In 1789, France had a form of elected **assembly** called the Estates-General. It met only when the king asked it to. That assembly had three separate groups, called estates. The nation's wealthy people formed one estate, while church officials formed another. France's king and the members of these two groups often had similar interests. They worked together to oppose the views of the majority of the French people. These people made up the Third Estate.

In 1789, the Third Estate broke away from the Estates-General and declared itself a new national assembly for the entire country. The leaders of the assembly wanted to greatly reduce the king's power and write a constitution. By 1792, France had a constitution that let all men vote. This ended the old, unethical practice of requiring voters to own a certain amount of property.[8]

Angry that the government ignored their rights, the French people arrested King Louis XVI and executed him in 1793.

Violence and voting today

In very recent history, revolutions demanding democracy have continued. Egypt, the Middle East's largest country by population, saw a series of protests begin in January 2011. Tens of thousands of people were angry about the economy and the growing gap between the rich and poor.[9]

Many were also upset with the government. One man, Hosni Mubarak, had ruled for 30 years. Egypt had elections, but they were largely considered rigged, or decided in advance in an unfair way. In 2010, for example, Mubarak's **party** won hundreds of seats in the country's parliament. Parties that opposed him won just 20. As the protests went on, Mubarak finally agreed to leave office. Egyptians soon made plans for their first free elections in decades.[10]

WAEL GHONIM (BORN 1980)

Setting up a Facebook page made Wael Ghonim a hero. Ghonim worked in Egypt for the Internet company Google. He set up the page in June 2010, to draw attention to the killing of a businessman by Egyptian police. It was thought he had evidence of police **corruption**, and so the police did not want the information released. Under President Mubarak, the Egyptian police often used extreme violence and acted corruptly.[11]

As the protests began, Egyptians used Ghonim's page to discuss their plans and call for democracy. For a time, Egypt shut down the Internet. But people still found ways to communicate with each other, relying on their cell phones. Ghonim was arrested during the protests, but was freed after 12 days in jail.[12] After he was released and Hosni Mubarak agreed to give up the presidency, Ghonim said, "This is the Internet Revolution."[13]

A spreading uprising

The Egyptian protests came after similar ones in Tunisia, another North African nation. The desire to have representative democracies quickly spread across the Middle East. Protests flared in Bahrain, Libya, and Syria. In each case, the ruling leaders resisted giving up power. And in each nation, people—many of them young—risked their lives in the name of political change.

What do you think?

At times, protesters in the Middle East broke their countries' laws to meet in public and call for a change in government. Is it ethical to break the law to seek fair elections and a truly democratic government?

In 2011, Egyptians filled Tahrir Square and other parts of the capital city of Cairo to demand democracy.

These people wanted to be able to elect their leaders in free and fair elections. In some cases, they were reacting to past unethical or illegal acts their leaders used to stay in power. The desire for political freedom is a strong force. And holding political power is a huge responsibility. Voting in free elections gives people the right to choose the best people to lead them, and to remove any who misuse the power they have been given.

DEMOCRACY IN ACTION

Today, most of the world's people live under some form of democratic government. Elections and voting are therefore at the center of most countries' governments, which have been built upon democratic models from throughout history.

Constitutions and elections

Most democracies have many things in common, including a constitution. A constitution is usually a written document that outlines the structure of a government and the most basic rights granted to citizens. For some countries, this includes information on who can run for elected office and who can vote.

Voters themselves usually have a say in writing or approving constitutions. This can happen through an election called a **referendum** or through representatives they elect. In 2011, the North African kingdom of Morocco had a referendum to approve a new constitution. Voters backed the constitution, which gave more power to the country's **prime minister**.[1]

Problems with counting the ballots in Florida led to a delay in naming the new U.S. president during the 2000 election.

Not all constitutions, however, are written. The United Kingdom has an unwritten constitution. Over time, laws passed by Parliament and decisions written by judges have created the framework for the country's government. The unwritten constitution also includes acts that have become accepted over time, without any one branch of government declaring them legal. The monarch's signing of a law passed by both houses of Parliament is one of these unwritten acts.[2] Having a constitution and written laws that apply equally to all means voters know what is legal and ethical in the electoral process.

The rule of law

Democracy is based on the notion of the rule of law, an idea passed down from ancient Rome (see page 7). All laws—including those in a constitution—apply the same to everyone, and anyone who breaks a law will be punished. U.S. and British legal thinkers have sometimes used the phrase "a government of laws and not men," to express this notion.[3] In other words, no one person, no matter how wealthy or powerful, is above the law.

"Government without a constitution is power without right."[4]

Thomas Paine, British political writer

The rule of law in action

The 2000 U.S. presidential election was one of the most controversial in the country's history. Both Vice President Al Gore and Texas governor George W. Bush needed the state of Florida's **electoral votes** to win the presidency. In some **polling stations**, however, voters had trouble using the electronic ballots. In some stations where paper punch cards were used, many of the cards didn't work properly (see photo at left).

Gore feared some votes meant for him were not properly counted. He asked for and received a recount of the votes by hand in some counties. At this point, Bush had a tiny lead over Gore. Bush supported the state official in charge of elections, who said the recount should be stopped—with Bush ahead.

The U.S. Supreme Court, the most powerful court in the country, finally settled the matter. The Court ruled in favor of Bush. Gore and his supporters were not happy that the recount was stopped, especially because Gore had won more popular votes across the country. Gore disagreed with the Court's decision, but he accepted it—because he accepted the rule of law. He said, "That's the ruling principle of American freedom, the source of our democratic liberties."[5]

Three branches today

All modern representative democracies usually have a similar system. It builds upon the ancient Roman example of three separate branches of government (see page 6): the executive, the legislative, and the judicial.

Voters directly elect most lawmakers. Executives can be directly elected, such as the presidents of various countries. They can also be chosen based on which party controls the parliament, as in the United Kingdom (see below). Voters and the people they elect usually belong to political parties. The parties are formed around certain shared values and ideas about how governments should be run. (For more on parties, see pages 18 to 27.)

Only three countries—Japan, Switzerland, and the United States—allow for the election of judges. Supporters of judicial elections say they give voters more influence in the government process. But opponents of those elections believe judges should not be concerned with winning popular support. Rather, they should simply follow the law. Judges might be influenced to do what is popular if they have to rely on voters to keep their jobs.[6]

Parliamentary systems

Today, many countries use a parliamentary system similar to the United Kingdom's "Westminster model." In this system, voters elect the members of the lower house of parliament.[7]

Members of the lower house are elected in different ways in different countries. The United Kingdom uses what is called the "first past the post" system. This means the person with the most votes wins, no matter how many people are running or how many votes are cast. In an election, each voting district chooses one member to represent it. The person with the most votes wins for that region and goes to represent his or her district in the UK Parliament.

The party with the most representatives in the lower house forms the government. These elected officials choose the executive, the prime minister.[8] Most parliaments and legislatures also have an upper house. These members can be either elected or appointed.

Other parliamentary systems use what is called **proportional representation**. In this system, political parties receive the number of seats in parliament that roughly equals the proportion of votes they won across the country.[9]

Some countries with "first past the post" voting systems	Some countries with proportional representation voting systems
Bangladesh Belize Botswana Canada France (two rounds of voting) Gambia India Malaysia Uganda United Kingdom Zambia	Albania Chile Denmark Finland Iraq Italy Morocco Romania Sweden Switzerland Turkey

Source: http://aceproject.org/epic-en/CDTable?question=ES005&set_language=en

Other systems

The United States has another model of representative democratic government. In elections for the national legislature, called **Congress**, lawmakers are elected in a "first past the post" method. Voters also choose the president, the head of the executive branch. But this is done through electoral votes by the states.

The U.S. structure is known as a federal system. This means the national government also shares power with the states. Other countries with federal governments include Australia, Canada, and Germany.

HOW DOES IT AFFECT ME?

What is the voting age where you live? Will you go to the polls the first year you are old enough to vote? Why or why not?

15

Creating new electoral systems

After revolutions or struggles, many countries move from other political systems toward democracy, which means voting and elections. But how can a new democracy be achieved? Choosing the best forms of democracy raises important ethical issues.

Creating a constitution gives a new nation or one with a new government a chance to shape its electoral system. That, in turn, determines how people will choose their representatives. The system chosen should reflect the social and political needs of the particular nation.[10] A "first past the post" voting system tends to make the winner of the vote more responsive to the people he or she serves. That might be important if corruption was a feature of the previous government.

In 2011, some South Sudanese voters waited in long lines to cast their vote for independence.

A proportional representation system, however, might be better in a country that has a history of racial or **ethnic** conflict. This was the case in South Africa, which had a history of brutal white rule over a black majority. Under a system called apartheid, black South Africans had few political rights and were forced to live apart from whites.

In South Africa's first truly democratic election in 1994, voters chose members of the new legislative body. The largest party for blacks, the African National Congress, won about 63 percent of the vote. This gave them the same percentage of seats in the assembly.[11] Having an assembly that reflected the views of the majority of the nation was seen as a way to ensure a stable society after years of racial violence.[12]

South Sudan:
Building a new democracy

In January 2011, voters in southern Sudan, in Africa, chose to secede (break off) from the rest of Sudan. The north and the south had been battling each other in a civil war for decades. The desire to control oil discovered in the south played a part in the war.

With the January vote, the world's newest nation was born: the Republic of South Sudan. Government leaders then had the difficult task of creating a constitution, which also included choosing an electoral system.

Many African nations had already received their independence during the 1960s. In some cases, they borrowed their electoral systems from the European nations that had once ruled them. But elections expert Robert Gerenge said the South Sudanese had "arguably, relatively more latitude [freedom] in terms of...choices" than these earlier countries.[13]

Members of more than 20 political parties in South Sudan met in April 2011 to discuss the constitution. In July, lawmakers passed a temporary constitution while planning to create a permanent one.[14] Writing a constitution gives a country a chance to make sure it has a free and fair election system that is acceptable to the greatest number of people. But with so many electoral systems to choose from, compromise can be hard.

THE ROLE OF PARTIES

Social Democrat, Republican, Christian Democrat, United Nationalist, Communist, **Conservative**, Green, **Liberal**—these are just some of the names people around the world use to describe themselves and their political beliefs. These terms all refer to various political parties.

In modern democracies, political parties are a key part of both the election process and governing. Parties bring together people who share similar views on important issues. All members, though, might not agree with each other on every issue. Parties also choose candidates who run for office and will seek to carry out the party's **platform** if elected. On Election Day, voters can vote for the candidate or the party that most closely matches their own beliefs.[1]

Parties also have a role to play in making sure government is ethical. Parties that do not hold power closely watch the activities of the ruling party. In parliamentary systems, the parties out of power are sometimes called the loyal **opposition**. They might oppose the ruling party, but they want what is best for the country.

Russian political battles: Challenging a leader in court

Russia is one of the world's largest democracies. But one man, Vladimir Putin, has had strong influence over the government for many years. In 2010, he made comments about key opposition leaders. Putin said these three men had stolen billions of rubles, the Russian currency, when they had earlier served in government. He said the three would steal again if they were allowed back into government. This led the accused men to sue Putin for slander. This crime involves publicly lying about others.

Boris Nemtsov, one of the three men, wanted Putin to apologize and pay a fine. If they won, Nemtsov and the opposition leaders wanted to use the money to inform Russians about corruption under Putin. In 2011, however, their lawsuit was thrown out of court. Some experts on Russian government were surprised the case even reached a court, given Putin's power.[2]

Political parties often take part in or help organize public events to do with key issues of the day. This London rally protested cuts in government spending.

In any system, the "out" or opposition parties can challenge government actions that are unethical. They can bring public attention to these actions, so that voters know the facts and will perhaps vote out the ruling party in the next election. Out parties also sometimes bring lawsuits to try to punish past illegal actions or prevent illegal acts from occurring. They also make sure the views of people outside the ruling party are still heard in legislative bodies.

The emergence of modern parties

Political parties have a long history. Starting in the 17th century, England developed a vibrant representative democracy. But the idea of political parties was not popular with most government leaders. By the 18th century, British parties were called factions—and factions were thought to be dangerous to good government. Political thinkers at the time believed that lawmakers should reach consensus, or agreement, with each other to do what was best for the nation. They should not promote the views of a certain group of people, as factions or parties did. They worried that loyalty to a party instead of the country would weaken the nation.[3]

Creating parties

Although some leaders opposed them, parties still developed. People who share similar views tend to come together. Working together to support a political candidate with those views was natural. In general, parties have always tried to appeal to voters on an ethical level—they assert that their platform will benefit the country or defend the rights of people not currently served by the political process.

Economics also often played a part, as one party might represent business owners, while another looks out for workers. In colonies such as India, parties sometimes formed around the notion of independence. That country's Congress Party was created in the 19th century to seek independence from the British Empire. It is still a major party in India today.[4] Modern parties have also been formed by members of a particular religious or ethnic group, such as Israel's Shas Party. This party represents the views of deeply religious Israelis who have roots in the Middle East.[5]

HOW DOES IT AFFECT ME?

What party or parties currently control the national government where you live? Does the same party also control the local government? Is there a policy of the national ruling party that affects you or someone in your family?

The Republican Party:
From the old, something new

Throughout the world, the first parties formed naturally among like-minded people. But at times, members of existing parties have decided to come together and create a new party. The leaders of the different parties realize they share some similar goals and can earn more votes by working together.

This happened in the United States during the 1850s. Slavery was dividing the nation, and it was becoming a major issue in national elections. The country was splitting, in large degree, along geographic lines. A growing number of Northerners were opposing the spread of slavery, while some wanted to end it altogether. Most slave states were in the South, and Southerners tended to support slavery. In 1854, northern members of the two major parties, the Whigs and Democrats, united with members of two smaller parties. Their union created the Republican Party, which focused on stopping the spread of slavery.

The Republicans are still one of the two major parties in the United States. The party changed its focus, though, once slavery ended. It began to concentrate on helping businesses grow and keeping taxes low. Any party can change its goals over time, as it responds to changes in the world and the shifts in its members' beliefs.

A Maori Party leader addresses a crowd in Wellington, the capital of New Zealand. The party looks out for the interests of the country's Maori people.

Powerful leaders

Parties often form around a distinct system of thought, called an **ideology**. Members of the party have faith that their ideology and the political system they promote is best for their nation. It is viewed as an issue of ethics, or right versus wrong.

At times, one person emerges to state an ideology and lead a party. During the early 1930s, Adolf Hitler and the Nazi Party used an ethical voting system to rise to power in Germany. Once the Nazis were in power, however, they began an unethical and violent rule. Hitler's ideology included killing people he considered inferior to Germans, such as Jews and Slavs.

One-party systems

After Hitler became chancellor (similar to a prime minister), Germany then outlawed all parties except the Nazi Party and ended elections. Some other parties that rule based on ideology have done the same thing. These are called **one-party systems**.

The most common examples of one-party systems have come in communist countries. The Soviet Union was a union of republics led by Russia that existed from 1922 to 1991. It called itself a democracy and made a great point of saying all voters went to the polls on Election Day. An army of government officials traveled across the country, making sure everyone went out to vote. At one time, a person who refused to vote could go to jail. But only the names of people approved by the ruling Communist Party could run, and the elected assembly had no power.[6]

Getting the vote

Adolf Hitler appealed to Germans who believed the country had suffered greatly after its loss in World War I (1914–1918). He promised to make the country powerful and respected again.

To do this, Hitler and his aides relied on propaganda. This is false or misleading information that tries to convince people of something. The Nazis used simple slogans and images to spread Hitler's message. One message was that Germans were naturally better than other people. Another was that the country had many enemies, and only Hitler and the Nazis could defeat them. Hitler told people what they wanted to hear or believe, and so they voted for his party. But all along, he planned to end democracy once he came to power.[7]

A Chinese voter casts a ballot in a local election. In 2011, independent candidates there won local elections for the first time.

China: A modern one-party system

The People's Republic of China is today's largest one-party system in the world. By law, any Chinese citizen over 18 years of age can vote and run for an elected office, unless he or she has been convicted of a crime. In reality, though, the average voter can only choose officials at the village level. For other levels of government, the Communist Party controls who will run for office. Even in the village elections, some Chinese say, the winner is arranged in advance. The party chooses the top leaders, with no general election at all.

When protests spread through North Africa in 2011, the Chinese government feared similar protests. It began to arrest anyone who might criticize the dominance of the Communist Party.[8]

WHAT DO YOU THINK?

Should a person go to jail rather than vote in an unfair election that offers only one candidate? What would be a possible reason for risking arrest rather than voting?

Creating and organizing parties

Around the world, new political parties form all the time. Egypt, for example, saw the creation of several new parties in 2011, after Hosni Mubarak left power (see pages 10 and 11). Under his rule, only parties he approved of could be formed.[9]

When the Soviet Union ended in 1991, this led to the creation of 15 new countries. Most saw a number of new political parties emerge. In several of these nations, however, one-party rule effectively remained in place.[10]

Russia: Struggles of a new party

As recently as 2011, Russian leaders prevented a new party they opposed from taking part in elections. The government said it found problems with the papers the People's Freedom Party submitted to become a legal party. The party did not follow rules for how leadership should change over time. The government also claimed that the names of dead people and people too young to vote were on the list of party members.

People's Freedom Party leaders said their structure was the same as that of other parties in the country. And while it might have made some mistakes in listing party members, it did have tens of thousands of real voters as members. The People's Freedom Party said its goal was to fight corruption in the Russian government. The party and other critics of the ruling party saw the government's actions as unethical. The ruling party wanted to silence critics and deny voters a true choice.[11]

What do you think?

Some nations, such as the United Kingdom and Lithuania, require a party to pay a fee to register.[12] Such a fee could keep out groups that are not serious about the political process and just want to draw attention to themselves. But some people who are serious about forming a party might be poor and have trouble paying a fee. Should parties be required to pay a fee to be placed on ballots?

Countries also have a wide range of rules for who can run for office. Most require that candidates be citizens of the country, and there is usually a minimum age, depending on the office.[13] Most countries also allow candidates to run without joining a party, although some will not let independent candidates run for president. Countries that follow this rule include Israel, Sweden, and Uruguay.[14]

Members of the Labour Party in Wales hold signs supporting their party, written in both English and Welsh.

Minimum age for becoming a member of the lower house of legislature	
Country	**Age**
Australia	18
Bahrain	30
Canada	18
Gabon	28
Iraq	30
Pakistan	25
Russia	21
Tanzania	21
United Kingdom	18
United States	25

What can I do?

Even if you are not close to the legal voting age in your country, you can begin to learn about the various parties and their platforms. Then, when you are old enough, you can make an informed decision about which party is best for you.

Party loyalty

One thing party leaders count on is loyalty from members. Party volunteers and donors are sometimes rewarded for their service. Under a system called **patronage**, loyal members receive jobs from other members who have control over the hiring in some government departments.

This was a feature of the so-called political machines that developed in some U.S. cities during the 19th and 20th centuries. Party members who rounded up voters for the party could expect a job. Even the voters themselves found work for their loyalty, or money to help with emergencies.[15] This system has sometimes been called clientilism, and it is still practiced in some countries, including Brazil and Mexico.[16]

Tammany Hall was a famous political machine in 19th-century New York City. The sign shows the machine's disappointment with the results of the 1884 presidential election.

Critics of patronage say it is unethical. People without the proper skills often receive important government jobs. To curb patronage, many governments now give jobs based on tests that prove a person's skills.

Parties and corruption

Most scholars of democracy say parties are essential to electing officials.[17] Still, parties can be a source of unethical behavior. Some voters think party leaders and elected officials take actions that benefit themselves or the party, but not the country as a whole. In 2011, in Ghana, in West Africa, government official Joseph Whittal pointed out some of the corruption issues his country faced. Some parties were demanding high fees from people who received jobs from the parties' members. In other cases, people were offering to pay money to be named as a candidate.[18]

Despite some political corruption in their homeland, voters in Ghana have taken part in several democratic elections in recent years.

A problem with patronage

In 2005, Hurricane Katrina roared ashore in the United States. Large sections of New Orleans, Louisiana, were particularly hard hit.

The Federal Emergency Management Agency (FEMA) is the part of the U.S. government in charge of helping citizens during disasters. At the time, the agency's leader was Michael Brown. He was a friend of someone close to President George W. Bush. That connection seemed to be what gave Brown the job, since he had no experience in disaster management.

Soon after the hurricane struck, Brown wrote in one e-mail, "Can I quit now? Can I come home?"[19] In another, he seemed not to realize the extreme conditions in New Orleans. President Bush supported Brown and his actions for several days. But Brown finally quit when critics said the government had failed to respond properly to the crisis. To some people, the incident suggested the dangers of patronage and people without the proper skills being given important government positions.

Various international groups are trying to end corruption and other unethical acts by parties. A group called the International Institute for Democracy and Electoral Assistance (IDEA) has drafted a code of conduct for parties. The rules in the code are voluntary. Still, the group hopes that once parties agree to follow them, countries will then give them the force of law. The code says parties should respect the rights of other parties to carry out **campaigns**. Party leaders are also expected to guarantee that all party members follow the code.[20] In 2011, 19 political parties in Thailand agreed to follow rules based on International IDEA's code.[21]

CAMPAIGNS

A candidate walks through a crowd, greeting the people pushing close to her. A radio ad stresses the good things an **incumbent** has done—or the bad things his opponent supports. Donors attend a dinner after paying large amounts of money for a ticket, knowing the funds will support the candidate holding the event.

All these activities are part of campaigning in many countries. A campaign is an important part of the electoral process. Campaigns give candidates a chance to share their views with voters. In turn, voters get the chance to see which candidate best addresses their interests. Campaigns, however, can also require a lot of money to run, especially at the national level (see pages 32 and 33). The amount of money raised in politics is one of the main concerns of people who oppose corruption. Other ethical issues in campaigns include who parties choose to represent them in elections—do the candidates truly reflect the views of local party members? And what candidates say about each other can also raise concerns. Truth sometimes is ignored as a candidate seeks to win a race.

Candidates for local offices must go where the voters are. Here, Chicago mayor Rahm Emanuel greets one as she prepares to board a train.

Different campaigns

Around the world, campaigns can vary from country to country, depending on local laws. In Japan, for example, a law written long before the creation of the Internet strictly limits how candidates can spread their message to voters. As a result, candidates in races for national offices cannot update their websites once a campaign begins.[1] But the rules there are different when a party holds its own elections to choose party officials. In 2010, candidates for the leadership of the Democratic Party of Japan used Twitter to send information to the party members voting.[2]

What do you think?

Is it right to keep campaigning off the Internet? How might this affect people who rely on the Internet for their news, as opposed to people who read newspapers or watch television?

Countries also have campaigns of various lengths. Countries with a parliament usually have short campaigns. In the United Kingdom and Australia, campaigns for national offices last about six weeks. France's election for president is even shorter.[3]

The longest campaigns occur for some national offices in the United States. Before the 2012 presidential election, held in November, several people announced they were candidates about 18 months before the election. Fundraising for the race began even earlier.[4] Regional and local elections might have limits on how a candidate can campaign for offices in those areas.

Becoming a candidate

Parties in different countries have different ways of choosing their candidates. Most countries allow parties to set up their own rules for how they choose candidates.[5] The system can start at the local level, even for offices in the national government. Most countries with parliaments have a similar system. Local party members either directly or indirectly choose who will represent them in an election.

But in some countries, such as Japan, national party leaders greatly influence who will be chosen to represent the party. These leaders choose the candidate for even the lowest offices. Then, these party members go to special classes to learn how to run for office. The leaders seek candidates who will closely follow the party's values.[6] At times, though, some party leaders might work against their own party's candidates. This can happen when personal or political differences split a party at a local level. Working against a chosen candidate or helping another party's candidate would be unethical.

Whom to choose?

Party leaders and committees that nominate (choose and promote) candidates look at different traits to decide who should represent the party. Do the candidates speak well and seem likable? Are they loyal to the party's values? Do they have the proper education or skills for the position? Some parties might also want to appeal to certain groups likely to vote in a certain race. Candidates from a certain racial, ethnic, or religious background might be thought to have a better chance of winning.

Some countries even set aside seats in their governments for members of certain groups. In India, there are seats for members of certain tribes. Macedonia is one of several nations that have seats just for women.[7] This practice is called positive discrimination, and it is meant to overcome the problems certain groups once had being represented in assemblies. Some people, however, question the fairness of positive discrimination. The practice selects some groups over others for special treatment, which seems to go against democratic values.[8]

Deliberative polling

As parties decide the fairest way to choose their candidates, the Greek party Pasok looked to the past. In 2006, Pasok used a method once used in ancient Athens for settling important issues.

Back then, several hundred citizens were chosen randomly to serve on juries and decide what topics all citizens would vote on. Pasok used a similar method to choose a local candidate for mayor. The party picked 160 members at random to choose among six possible candidates. The voters received information on all six and had a chance to question them directly. The voters then discussed what they learned and voted for their favorite.

The process, called deliberative polling, was developed at Stanford University in California, based on the idea of ancient direct democracy (see page 6). Supporters of the process say it gets voters more involved in political decisions, such as choosing a candidate.[9]

Barack Obama used the Internet to raise money and attract voters during both the 2008 and 2012 U.S. presidential elections.

Who can run?

In representative democracies, anyone can run for office, as long as they meet any legal requirements for age and citizenship. That notion, however, is sometimes hard to put into practice. Not only do most candidates need the support of a party. They also need to raise money.

The world's most expensive campaigns are in the United States. For his campaign in 2008, President Barack Obama spent almost $750 million, and he raised even more for his reelection campaign in 2012.[10]

The importance of money

A U.S. politician once said, "Money is the mother's milk of politics."[11] He meant that money is the one essential thing politicians need to run a campaign.

The role of money is also a large source of corruption in politics. Candidates sometimes break the law, or come close to it, to get money. And a variety of people or groups with money—for example, businesses, wealthy individuals, and **unions**—donate with the hope of gaining something in return. In the United Kingdom, some donors have given money to parties in hopes of receiving a knighthood, a high honor.[12] In some cases, the donors seek influence in the political process.

Many campaign laws about finances are meant to limit what is called a **conflict of interest**. Politicians who receive a lot of money from one source might do what that donor wants, rather than what is best for voters.

Money and ethics

The cost of running for office presents some of the most challenging ethical questions in politics. Parties need money to pay for ads and the people who run campaigns. There is no way to end the need for money in democratic elections.[13]

But some people ask: Is it fair that one party or candidate can raise and spend more than another? Is it good for democracy if millionaires can use their own money on a campaign, as happens in some countries? Many people say no. One solution, some believe, is for candidates to use public funding.

"When you go to Congress, half the sitting members are millionaires... so you get people who don't have the day to day concerns of the average American, and that's scary if you want a representative government."

Nick Nyhart, U.S. political reformer

Public funding

A system of public funding limits donations candidates receive. It also gives more money to some candidates if their opponents spend large amounts of their own money.[14] More than 150 countries around the world have some sort of public funding of candidates, to make sure politics and government are not controlled by the wealthy.[15]

But not everyone supports public funding. Critics say taxpayers should not be forced to support political parties they disagree with—especially if it means less money for things they want, such as education or health care. And parties might rely on the government money and make less of an effort to reach out to average voters on a direct level, as they do when seeking funds.[16]

Most countries also address the funding issue with laws on private donations. Companies and private individuals might be limited on how much they can give. In some countries, such as Canada and Israel, companies cannot donate at all. And many countries also ban or limit donations from foreign residents and companies.[17]

Types of public funding for political parties around the world	
Type of public funding	**Number of nations**
Equal for all political parties	43
Based on the party's results in the previous election	68
Based on the number of seats the party holds in the legislature	41
Based on the number of candidates running in the current election	17

Source: http://aceproject.org/epic-en/CDTable?question=PC015&set_language=en

How does it affect me?

Even if you cannot vote yet, you might be able to work for a candidate's campaign. Candidates rely on volunteers to work in offices and spread printed material about their views. It is a great way to learn about the campaigning process from the inside! Before volunteering, research a candidate's views to make sure they match your values.

Fans and followers

In many countries, the government requires candidates to keep track of who donates to their campaign and how much they give. Parties must also keep track of this information. The information is then publicly available, so anyone can see who supports which candidate. With this knowledge, the public can better tell if a politician has a conflict of interest.

With an incumbent, voters can track the person's voting habits and compare it to the list of donors. Does the person usually vote for laws that favor the interests of a major company or wealthy donor? If so, are the laws ones that most people in the district oppose? Voters can organize to work against candidates that seem to favor their donors' interests rather than the public good.

Knowing how candidates get their money is part of **transparency**. This idea refers to making the political process as open and visible as possible. Voters need the most information they can get about candidates and the process to make the best choices. By 2009, however, dozens of countries still did not have laws that called for disclosing donations to candidates.[18] The United Nations and other international groups continue to work for greater transparency in elections around the world.

PACs: Money for votes?

Despite legal limits on donations, some donors and politicians look for ways to keep the money flowing. In the United States, **political action committees (PACs)** are one source of large donations. A company or organization can start a PAC. So can a group of people who support a particular cause, such as protecting the environment.

Critics say public officials who receive PAC money are more likely to pass laws the PACs want. In 2011, PACs created by U.S. oil companies gave more than $1 million to members of Congress who supported their interests. Specifically, the lawmakers voted to allow the oil companies special tax breaks (tax conditions more favorable to the companies). Only $45,000 went to lawmakers who opposed the tax breaks. Supporters of PACs say the groups give people a chance to work together to support a candidate, which is their legal right.[19]

International experts say no country has perfectly addressed financial transparency. At times, the problem comes down to free speech issues. In some countries, donating money and spending freely on political ads are seen as part of protected speech. Lawmakers and courts have to balance that right with trying to keep elections free and fair.

U.S. campaigns: Money and free speech

In 2010, the U.S. Supreme Court gave a huge legal victory to large companies with its ruling in *Citizens United v. Federal Election Committee*. The Court said the government could not limit how much companies spend during political campaigns. It said that donations to support a candidate are a form of free speech, and companies have the same rights to free speech as a person. Justice Anthony Kennedy noted that "speech is an essential mechanism of democracy, for it is the means to hold officials accountable to the people."[20]

The decision upset some Americans. They believed that the largest companies could spend more than citizens to influence an election. President Barack Obama said the decision was "a major victory for powerful interests that marshal their power every day in Washington to drown out the voices of everyday Americans."[21]

In presidential campaigns around the world, candidates spend money for ads in newspapers, as well as on TV and radio.

35

Corruption on the campaign trail

Along with laws that limit how much one group or person can give, some candidates choose to limit the size and kind of donations they receive. They want to show voters they are not likely to be influenced by donations. In some countries, however, candidates have willingly taken money from illegal sources. The problem has arisen several times in Latin America. In Colombia, for example, drug dealers have made large donations to political campaigns. In return they expected elected officials to ignore their illegal activities.[22] Members of a Colombian rebel group named FARC have also donated to candidates. The rebels have ties to illegal drug dealing.[23] In 2011, evidence emerged linking the group to Ecuador's president, Rafael Correa. The president, however, denied knowingly receiving money from FARC.[24]

Legal donations, illegal use

At times, the source of a politician's money might be legal, but how it is used might not be. In 2008, Israeli Prime Minister Ehud Olmert faced charges that several years before he had illegally taken money from a U.S. businessman. Olmert said the money was strictly for campaign expenses. But police charged that he used some of the money for personal items. Israeli officials say Olmert did not report the money, as required by law, and that he tried to help the donor make government connections that would aid his business. The charges in this case and other financial **scandals** forced Olmert to resign from office.[25]

Dirty tricks

Money is not the only source of unethical action during a campaign. For hundreds of years, candidates have sometimes tried to damage their opponents' reputations. These tactics are sometimes called dirty tricks. Candidates, or people working for them, might spread rumors about another candidate. The rumors often accuse the person of doing something illegal. Or the politicians might carry out illegal acts as part of their dirty tricks.

Downfall of a president

In 1972, U.S. president Richard Nixon was running for re-election as the candidate of the Republican Party. He and some of his aides broke the law that year when they approved a plan to break into the headquarters of the rival Democratic Party. The aim was to leave listening devices in the office, so Nixon would know what the Democrats were planning for the campaign.

The burglars, however, were arrested. The break-in took place at an office building called the Watergate, and for two years Nixon tried to deal with what was called the Watergate scandal. Publicly, he denied knowing anything about the break-in. But in secret, he was trying to hide the links between the burglars and his re-election team. Thanks to the reporting of a Washington newspaper, the truth about Nixon's role came out. With the evidence against him growing, Nixon chose to resign rather than face **impeachment** (see page 51). He is the only U.S. president to leave office because of a scandal.

Richard Nixon (right) leaves the White House for the last time as U.S. president. With Nixon's resignation, Vice President Gerald Ford (left) took over the presidency.

THE ROLE OF THE MEDIA IN VOTING AND ELECTIONS

To spread their campaign messages, candidates and parties rely on the **media**. Newspapers, television and radio networks, and political websites all closely watch campaigns. The media report what candidates say and do. At their best, these reports give voters information they need to choose their candidates. With the issues they focus on, the media can also shape the topics that voters will care about and investigate for themselves.

Political reporting

But in some countries, the media is faulted for how they cover elections. They might not examine the truth of what candidates say or explore how their plans will actually affect voters. In the United States, critics say the media should spend less time on the "horse race"—meaning which candidate is leading in opinion polls—and more on the issues.

Several reports have also shown that some candidates receive better treatment in the media than others. One candidate might receive more coverage than another, or the reports on certain candidates might stress problems they have in their campaigns. This **bias** sometimes reflects the views of the owners of a media company. They can use their reporting to help candidates they like and hurt ones they do not.[1]

RUPERT MURDOCH (BORN 1931)

Australian business owner Rupert Murdoch has built one of the largest media companies in the world. He also has strong conservative political views, and his companies often reflect that bias.

Because of the size of his companies and the influence the media have on politics, some people worry that Murdoch has too much power.[2] His papers and networks could present negative reports on politicians if they oppose his interests. The questions over Murdoch's power grew in 2011, when it was reported that one of his papers illegally obtained voicemails on private cell phones, and sometimes paid police officers for inside information. People were also worried about Murdoch's close relations with powerful political figures such as UK prime minister David Cameron and former prime minister Gordon Brown.[3]

CAMPAIGNS, AMERICAN STYLE

The various ads candidates use are often created by experts called consultants, who have a background in the media. U.S. consultants perfected the idea of selling candidates the same way ads sell goods. They appeal to the emotions and try to make the viewers feel good. This form of political advertising, however, also led to attack ads and stress-inducing sound bites (short bits of information). The candidates try to repeat their message over and over and not get away from the message they are trying to "sell."

This form of political consulting has gone international. In the United Kingdom, Prime Minister David Cameron and former prime minister Tony Blair are well known for using this approach. British author James Harding said this form of advertising does not address important issues. But with simple messages, candidates might draw out people who would otherwise not vote.[4]

Political advertising

How politicians use the media is often regulated during campaigns. Switzerland, for example, forbids all media advertising. Other countries allow candidates equal—and limited—free time on television. Some require candidates to pay for their television time.[5] In Germany, candidates can put up billboards promoting themselves for only a few weeks.[6]

The importance of television ads also varies from country to country. In poorer countries with fewer television sets, candidates might rely more on radio, posters, or newspapers.

Successful political candidates, such as Canada's Anne McLellan, must be comfortable speaking to members of the media.

Types of ads

Whatever media they use, candidates can take several directions with their ads. Some are informational. The ads try to explain who the candidates are and what policies they support.

In recent decades, so-called attack ads have become more common. Candidates or PACs (see page 34) that support them attack a specific opponent. Attack ads sometimes present a distorted view of the truth or simply lie to viewers.

For example, in 2004, one ad claimed that U.S presidential candidate John Kerry lied about details of his military record during the Vietnam War. Kerry was running against the incumbent, President George W. Bush. The charge was not true, but the ad still hurt Kerry's campaign.[7] Bush did not criticize the ad when it ran. He did not speak out against it until it was no longer shown.[8] In the meantime, he benefited from the bad image of Kerry it created.

In 1996, in the United Kingdom, the Conservative Party ran an ad showing Tony Blair, the Labour Party candidate, with red, demon-like eyes. The ad drew attention to the idea that Blair could not be trusted. Many political experts, however, thought the ad did not help the Conservative Party. In fact, it may have been so extreme that it actually hurt the party.[9]

What can I do?

Even if you cannot vote, you can follow a candidate or government official on Facebook or another form of social media and express your views on important issues.

French president Nicolas Sarkozy used Facebook to reach voters in his country.

The new media

The 21st century has seen the rise of Internet social media, such as Facebook, blogs, YouTube, and Twitter. These have become an important part of political campaigns. Politicians at all levels of government reach out to voters through social media.

In the 2010 UK election, both major parties placed ads and took part in chats on a popular social networking website geared toward mothers.[10] Once elected, some politicians also communicate with voters through social media.

But politicians are not the only ones turning to social media to become active in elections and government. In Nepal, leaders of the country's political parties were supposed to write a new constitution for the country in 2010. By 2011, the parties had not acted, and young voters upset with the delay went to the Internet. They created a Facebook page demanding that the parties take action. The page also helps spread news about public protests of the slow pace of drafting the constitution.[11]

"We are not trying to derail the political process...because we all are believers in democracy and liberal values. It is already democracy, we are just trying to strengthen it."[12]

Prashant Singh, a founder of the Facebook campaign in Nepal

ONLINE MONEY

In 2008, during his first campaign for president, Barack Obama showed the power of the Internet as a fundraising tool. Using his own website and a Facebook page, he received online donations of about $500 million from several million people.[13] These online funds then helped Obama set up offices that he used to make direct contact with more voters.[14] Thanks to the Internet, Obama was able to directly reach voters, instead of relying on his party, coverage in the traditional media, or television ads. His fundraising success has led politicians around the world to use social media during their campaigns.

VOTERS AND THE VOTING PROCESS

Voting is one of the greatest rights in a representative democracy. Who votes and how they vote determines the direction a country takes.

Through history, gaining **suffrage**, or the right to vote, has been the goal of many different groups. For a time, some countries limited suffrage to people who owned a certain amount of property. Many countries did not let women vote until the 20th century. And in some countries, certain ethnic, racial, or religious groups might have the legal right to vote but face obstacles to actually reaching the ballot box.

During the early part of the 20th century, women in Great Britain risked arrest as they demanded suffrage.

Limiting the vote in the United States

Even when people have a constitutional right to vote, some local governments have tried to disenfranchise voters, or take away that right. These efforts were particularly strong in some parts of the United States after slavery was outlawed in 1865.

Changes to the U.S. Constitution in 1870 said all males had the right to vote. (Women across the country did not win suffrage until 1920.) But in the South, state governments passed laws that made it hard for African Americans and some whites to vote. The states required poll taxes. This meant that voters had to pay money when they went to vote. Recently freed slaves often had little money, so they could not afford to pay the tax. Some states also introduced literacy tests. Voters had to prove they could read and write before they were allowed to vote.

People who were denied the right to vote thought the taxes and tests were not only unethical, but also illegal. They challenged the laws in court. Both poll taxes and literacy tests were finally outlawed across the United States in 1965. Still, in recent years some conservative politicians and writers have called for a different kind of literacy test for voters. They want voters to prove that they understand the Constitution and how governments work in the United States.[1]

Registering to vote

Before voters can go to the polls, they must register. In most democratic nations, the government requires people to register once they reach the voting age. Registering voters helps governments make sure that people are actually eligible to vote. It then makes it easier to track who has and has not voted on Election Day.[2]

Limits on voting today

Giving all adult residents the right to vote is called universal suffrage. But even with the historical trend to extend voting rights, some countries still have limits on voting. Nations set a minimum age—usually 18 or 21 years old. Most countries do not let people vote if they have been convicted of certain crimes, but a handful of nations let criminals vote without limits.[3]

Many nations also prevent the mentally disabled from voting. Historically, the thinking has been that people with some sort of mental disability cannot understand the issues and make educated decisions in the voting booth. One concern, though, has been deciding what "mentally disabled" means and who decides which people meet that definition. If electoral officials decide, they might not have the skills to know if a person's mental disability keeps him or her from being an informed voter. In 2006, the United Kingdom voted to give people with mental disabilities the right to vote. Canada, Ireland, and several other nations also guarantee that right.[4]

The most extreme limit on voting today might be in Saudi Arabia. Women there are not allowed to vote. In 2011, a group of women in the kingdom created a website demanding that right. Later that year, one part of the Saudi government called for letting women vote in the 2015 national elections. The king later approved this and said women would also be able to vote in local elections starting that year.[5]

Compulsory voting

In some countries, voting is not just a right—it is a legal duty. Several dozen nations require all people who are eligible to vote to go to the polls. A person who does not vote can be fined. But some countries with **compulsory** voting laws do not actively enforce them. These include Thailand and Bolivia.

People who support compulsory voting say having the most number of people possible vote is good for representative democracy. Being forced to vote might also make people more likely to educate themselves about important political issues. Opponents, though, say forcing someone to vote goes against the idea of freedom that is so important in a democracy. Having a political choice can mean choosing *not* to do something. And voters who are forced to vote might simply choose to leave their ballot blank, which really serves no purpose.[6]

Countries without compulsory voting laws often have many registered voters who do not go to the polls. And in countries where registering is voluntary, such as the United States, many people who could register choose not to do so.

What do you think?

Do people who have the legal right to vote have an ethical duty to use that right? Or would it be better for someone who is not informed about the issues and candidates not to vote?

Fewer voters

Over the years, voting rates have declined in many countries. In the United States, turnout rises and falls depending on the race. The turnout is much higher in years when a president is elected, compared to when only local races are being decided.[7] In the United Kingdom, 84 percent of registered voters voted in the 1950 elections for Parliament. That number has declined over the years, with just 66 percent voting in the 2010 election.[8]

Voter turnout in select countries for legislative elections			
Country	**Year**	**Voter turnout %**	**Compulsory voting law**
Australia	2010	93.2	Yes
Canada	2011	61.4	No
Chile	2009	87.7	Yes
Ethiopia	2010	93.4	No
France	2007	60	No
Indonesia	2009	71	No
Italy	2008	80.5	No
Mexico	2009	44.1	No
United Kingdom	2010	65.8	No
United States	2010	40.9	No

A group of women in Saudi Arabia gather outside a voter registration center to demand their right to vote in 2011.

Problems at the voting booth

Representative democracies follow the idea of "one person, one vote." The goal is to make sure that every eligible voter can reach the poll, and that each person votes just one time. These two issues are the major concerns for election officials. But both individuals and governments have tried to find ways to commit **fraud**.

One way for an individual to commit fraud is to use another person's name, in order to vote more than once. Some places try to limit this by requiring voters to show some form of identification. People caught trying to vote more than once can be fined or sent to jail. This type of fraud can also happen if someone asks for a mail-in ballot using another person's name.

Another type of fraud is ballot stuffing, or adding illegal ballots for one candidate. In Turkey's national election of 2011, some people were arrested for trying to use fake ballots.[9] Governments can also try to stuff ballot boxes. One way to avoid this is with laws that only let election officials place ballots in a ballot box.[10]

Election officials watch carefully as a woman votes during the 2011 elections in Turkey.

The "Australian" ballot: Privacy in voting

Voting in ancient Athens was public, but representative democracies today believe balloting should be secret. Secret ballots help reduce fraud.

This tradition started in the 19th century in Australia. Most voting at the time was public. Both there and in England, some voters worried that employers or other powerful people might influence how others voted. The powerful might try to punish someone who did not vote as they wanted. Also, election results were public while the voting went on. Everyone knew who was winning an election while it was happening. Because of this, candidates might look for people they could easily convince to vote for them.

To address these concerns, Australia decided to use a secret ballot. Sheets of paper had the candidates' names printed on them, and voters placed their completed ballot in a locked box. The votes were counted once the election was over. This system of secret voting is sometimes called the Australian ballot.[11]

Buying the vote

In some countries, candidates have tried to "buy" elections by paying people to vote a certain way. Thailand has a reputation for this kind of corruption, and it happened as recently as 2011.[12]

That same year, government documents from the United States said that India's ruling Congress Party had set aside money to buy the support of members of parliament. During Indian elections, voters have also received money to vote a certain way.[13]

In some U.S. cities, parties have sometimes given money or bought small goods for people who help get others to the polling station. This so-called walking-around money is usually spent in poor neighborhoods. Using this money is legal, as long as no one actually receives money for voting a certain way.[14]

Ensuring fair, legal elections is crucial for a democratic nation. If voters sense there is fraud or some other illegal actions, they could lose faith in their country's government.

Keeping watch at the polls

The effort to keep elections legal has many levels. It starts at the individual polling station, where local workers make sure voters are registered and that each person only votes once.

India is the world's largest democracy, with more than 71 million voters. Its Election Commission oversees about 5 million polling workers and police officers to make sure all elections are legal.[15]

On a larger level, observers from international organizations might keep watch over the stations or how votes are counted. These groups are more likely to get involved when a nation is newly democratic or facing some kind of violence.

During voting in Burundi, in eastern Africa, in 2010, United Nations (UN) officials watched over the election process.[16] The country had endured a long civil war and needed help proving to voters that the electoral process was transparent. But even with the UN presence, some candidates refused to take part in some elections. They thought fraud had occurred during earlier votes.[17]

UN soldiers watch as local election officials in East Timor carry out ballot boxes. The UN presence is designed to prevent voter fraud.

Forcing the vote in Turkey: Intimidation

The secret ballot (see page 47) was supposed to make it impossible for others to know how someone voted. But modern technology can get around that, if someone wants to use intimidation. With intimidation, parties or the ruling government use the threat of force or some other harm if a person does not vote a particular way.

This occurred during the 2011 Turkish election. Some voters were told to take pictures of their ballots with cameras in their cell phones. Then they were supposed to show the picture to the officials of a certain party, to prove they had voted for that party's candidates. The threat was that if they did not vote as the party told them to, the voters would face some sort of danger. Hearing rumors of this intimidation, voting officials told all voters not to take their phones with them into the voting booth.

Indiana: Identifying voters

In some U.S. states, lawmakers have required voters to show a government-issued photo identification (ID) before receiving a ballot to vote. Supporters of the IDs say they help cut down on voter fraud. But in many states, fraud has been a very small problem.

Since 2005, Indiana has been a legal battleground for a voter ID law. It was challenged in court because critics said that requiring an ID makes it hard for some citizens to use their right to vote. Particularly affected are the elderly, poor, and minorities (meaning groups, such as racial groups, that do not make up the majority of the population). Opponents say that these voters tend to vote more often for the Democratic Party, and most of the supporters of the ID laws are Republicans.

In 2008, the U.S. Supreme Court ruled that the Indiana voter ID law did not violate the U.S. Constitution. A voting rights group then challenged the law because it did not apply to all voters. People using absentee ballots did not have to show a picture ID. In 2010, an Indiana court rejected this claim. Not all the judges, however, agreed the law was constitutional. One said any changes to voting rights should be done by changing the state constitution, not merely passing a law.[18]

Referenda

When they go to the polls, voters choose representatives and leaders who will have a huge influence over their lives. But not all voting is about electing someone. Many nations allow voters to play a more direct role in creating or rejecting laws or shaping their nation's constitution. This kind of vote is called a referendum.

Across Europe, voters came out for referenda on whether or not to support the constitution of the European Union. This poster calls for a "yes" vote.

The recall

Along with offering laws for voters to accept or reject, some referenda also let voters remove elected officials. At times, officials can be **recalled** simply if they have lost public support. In other cases, there must be proof that the incumbent has done something wrong or is no longer physically or mentally able to do the job. The recall process usually starts with the collection of signatures of a certain number of registered voters. Once that is done, the actual referendum takes place.[19]

Many recall votes take place at the local level. But some countries allow recall votes for nationally elected figures. These include Ecuador, Ethiopia, and Nigeria. In these countries, and several others, voters begin the recall process. In others, government officials do so, and voters simply approve or reject the recall.[20]

Challenging a powerful president

In 1998, Hugo Chavez was elected president of Venezuela, in South America. During his presidency, Chavez began to assert his power in ways that some residents thought were unethical or illegal. Some election results raised questions of fraud. And in 2001, Chavez used special power he received from the legislature to pass laws that hurt the country's wealthiest citizens.

Chavez's opponents decided to call for a recall referendum to try to force Chavez out of office. The vote came in 2004. It was the first time in history a president faced a recall. In the end, Chavez won the vote. He also won re-election in 2006.[21]

Not everyone favors the use of recall votes. Opponents say elected officials should be allowed to serve their term. If voters do not like their policies, they can choose to vote for someone else in the next election. If elected officials break the law, the government can use the impeachment process to remove them (see box below).[22] Supporters say the recall gives voters a direct way to shape their government. Elected officials are more likely to listen to voters' concerns if they know the voters can remove them from office.[23]

The impeachment of Bill Clinton

In the United States, Bill Clinton was the last president to face impeachment. In 1998, Clinton was accused of lying during legal questioning, and of trying to limit an investigation into his actions. The investigation focused on Clinton's relations with two young women. As a result, he faced impeachment.

Impeachment in the United States is a two-step process. One half of Congress, the House of Representatives, formally charges someone with breaking the law or doing something unethical. Then the other half of Congress, the Senate, acts to decide if the person is guilty and should be removed from office. Clinton faced two charges. The Senate found him not guilty, and he remained in office.[24]

The final result

The voters have marked their ballots and the polls have closed. Now, the counting begins. In some cases, election officials must count the votes by hand. Other nations use computers to record and count the votes. In some cases, officials count the votes at each polling station. Other times, votes are brought to a central counting office. In either case, election officials must make sure all votes are counted properly. Once winners are declared, the elected officials go through some kind of ceremony to mark the beginning of their term of office.

Challenging the vote

As discussed on pages 46 and 47, fraud is a major concern, especially at polling stations. In 2010, Afghans saw examples of ballot stuffing and violence against election officials, as one party or another tried to influence the vote.[25] The country's election committee received about 6,000 complaints about the voting process. In some cases, all the votes at certain stations were thrown out, because officials could not guarantee they were accurate. It took the commission more than two months to announce all the winners.

Preventing fraud in India: In search of a "paper trail"

Many countries and regions have recently turned to electronic voting machines in an effort to reduce fraud. No one can stuff a computer with extra votes, and humans are not involved in the counting process. But some people still have a concern about potential problems with electronic voting.

In 2009, scientists showed that it was possible to hack, or gain entry to, voting machines and change the results. In response to this problem, some political parties in India called for using electronic voting machines that create a "paper trail." The machines record the votes both electronically and on paper. After voting, voters would be able to check the paper to make sure the machine correctly recorded their vote.

In 2011, India began testing some of these machines during a pretend election. Election Commission officials said the machines worked well. But another group said some voters did not receive the paper record of their votes. Election Commission officials said the problems could be fixed before the machines were used in real elections.

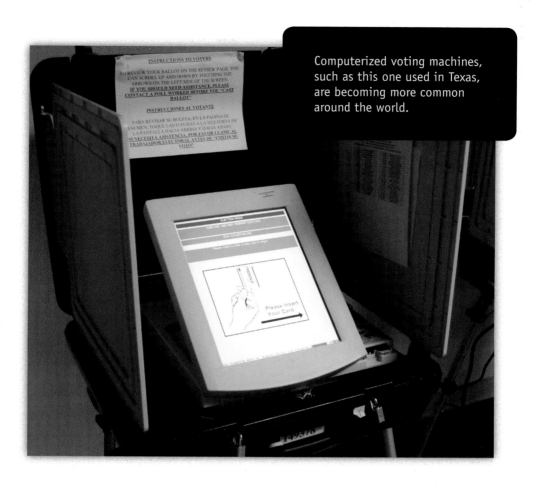

Computerized voting machines, such as this one used in Texas, are becoming more common around the world.

At times, candidates or parties might wage a legal challenge to election results, as in the 2000 U.S. presidential election (see page 13). Other times, a country might struggle to form a new government once members of parliament are elected. This happened in Iraq in 2010. No party won a majority, and the parties spent nine months debating how to distribute important positions such as prime minister and president.

Unfortunately, in some cases, election results can lead to violence. One party might feel that fraud was so massive that it cannot trust any legal solution. Or an incumbent who loses in a fair election may not want to give up power. In 2010, Alassane Ouattara won the presidency of Ivory Coast, a country in West Africa—a result that other nations accepted. But the ruling president, Laurent Gbagbo, refused to leave office. Into the next year, supporters of the two candidates fought each other, leading to hundreds of deaths.

VOTING AND ELECTIONS TODAY

Over thousands of years, people have developed different forms of government. Of these forms, representative democracies give voters the greatest chance to shape their lives. Through elections, people can express their views about the kind of society in which they want to live.

For most countries, using the ballot box leads to a peaceful change of government. Voters express their views by choosing certain representatives. The process is not always easy, and ethical violations do occur. But democracy has come to be the world's most popular form of government, and voting is one of the most precious human rights.

Different rights and duties

Elected officials are given great powers—whether it is to make laws or to see that laws are carried out. At times, the desire for that power can lead to corruption and fraud in the election process. Some candidates want to get elected at all costs. Some wealthy people want to shape the political process to suit their personal needs. Elected rulers might decide they no longer want to give voters a fair choice and want to remain in power.

The rule of law helps curb some of the unethical actions that can occur during campaigns and the voting process. Countries need to spell out what is and is not allowed. But governments must be willing to enforce the laws. At times, the media and independent groups must also play a part to make sure elections are transparent and fair.

Voters have a duty, too, to educate themselves about the candidates and the issues. Then when they are alone in the voting booth, they must choose the best people they can, based on what they know and the values they hold. Democracy gives people many rights and freedoms. Making voting and elections as ethical as possible helps guarantee that these freedoms are not taken away.

Some views on democracy, elections, and ethics

Read the quotations below. Based on what you have read in this book, decide if you agree or disagree with each writer. Choose one quotation that you disagree with and list some of the arguments you would make to challenge that view.

"We know that money always follows politics, in a variety of ways. But money politics can seriously undermine democracy because it [leads] elected leaders and politicians to serve their paymasters at the expense of the public good. It also produces an artificial democracy, one that betrays the public trust and crushes democratic ideals."—Susilo Bambang Yudhoyono, president of Indonesia

"Political campaigns are no longer targeting the...middle as much as the easily misled. Instead of intelligent debates about important topics such as health care reform and cash-strapped states, we have an exchange of easy to remember catchphrases such as 'Obamacare' and 'War on Unions.'"—U.S. journalist L. Z. Granderson

"The Democratic and Republican parties don't [care] about America. They put their parties first, and their political ambitions first. Their special interest, corporate donors first. We [voters] may be about fourth in line, but you know what? We can solve all that...stop voting for Democrats and Republicans...you know what they ought to have— how about the option of none of the above on the ballot?"—Jesse Ventura, former independent governor of Minnesota

"The involvement, the discussion, the debate, the spreading of information and the learning from experience can lead to change and improvement—and to citizens who value, support and engage with governance of their local communities and the decisions which affect their lives."—Andrew Ellis, International Institute for Democracy and Electoral Assistance (IDEA)

GLOSSARY

assembly group of people; specifically, the people elected to make laws for a country

ballot paper or card that voters mark during an election

bias view in favor or against something, often not directly stated

campaign series of actions taken by a candidate to win voter support before an election

candidate person seeking an elected office

colony territory controlled by a foreign nation

communist referring to a form of government in which the government owns many or most businesses and one political party has strict control over the citizens

compulsory required

conflict of interest situation in which people take actions that benefit themselves or others, while harming the public good

congress group of people called together for a special purpose; when capitalized, it refers to the lawmaking body of the United States

conservative tending to believe that the old ways of doing things are best; in politics, conservatives often oppose using the government to solve social or economic problems

constitution written document or unwritten rules that outline the structure of a government and the most basic rights granted to citizens

corruption actions that involve getting money or power illegally

democracy form of government in which voters directly make laws

democratic relating to a democracy

direct democracy form of government in which citizens discuss and vote on issues, such as laws, on their own, rather than through representatives

electoral vote vote counted in the United States to choose a president, based on which candidate wins the most ballots cast in each state

ethical relating to actions that are proper or good

ethics study of good and bad behavior, or the beliefs that shape that behavior

ethnic relating to groups of people who share the same national background

executive referring to the branch of government that carries out laws, or the person in charge of that branch

fraud act of lying or deceit

ideology system of belief, based on deeply held values, that serves as the basis for political action

impeachment political process used to remove some government officials from office after they are accused of doing something wrong

incumbent person who already holds a political office

judicial referring to the branch of government made up of courts and judges, which make sure laws are carried out fairly

legislative referring to the branch of government that makes laws

liberal tending to believe that government has an important role to play in solving social or economic problems

media organizations that gather and spread news, such as newspapers, TV stations, and websites

monarch ruler whose power to govern is passed on from a relative who once ruled

monarchy form of government with a king or queen whose power to rule is passed on to a relative when he or she dies

one-party system government in which only one political party controls the election process and rules the country

opposition party or parties that do not have control of a government

parliament branch of some governments that makes a country's laws

party political group whose members have similar beliefs and goals and try to elect people who represent their views

patronage giving of jobs or money in return for political support

platform specific laws and policies a candidate or party will support once in power

policy specific political belief or plan of action

political relating to politics and the actions of candidates to get elected

political action committee (PAC) organization created to raise money for a particular candidate, party, or political idea

politics system used for constructing a government and influencing how that government is run

polling station place where people vote

prime minister head of a government

proportional representation political system that gives a party a number of candidates in a parliament based on the total number of votes it receives in a nation

recall vote held to decide if an elected official should stay in office

referendum vote held to settle major issues, such as creating new laws or accepting a constitution

register sign up to do something, such as vote

representative democracy form of government in which people elect others to express their views and concerns

scandal illegal or unethical activity that creates unwanted public attention for someone

suffrage right to vote

transparency having the ability to be seen clearly

union workers who come together to seek better pay or working conditions

NOTES ON SOURCES

THE WILL OF THE PEOPLE (pp. 4–5)

1. Marc Santora, "Frustration Grows in Iraq at Slow Pace of Tally," *New York Times*, March 14, 2010, http://www.nytimes.com/2010/03/15/world/middleeast/15iraq.html?ref=elections05iraq.html.

2. *New York Times*, "Iraq," August 4, 2011, http://topics.nytimes.com/top/news/international/countriesandterritories/iraq/index.html.

3. United Nations, "UN Universal Declaration of Human Rights," https://www.un.org/en/documents/udhr/.

4. The CIA World Factbook, "Cuba," http://news.bbc.co.uk/2/hi/americas/46399.stm.

5. Gianfranco Baldini and Adriano Poppalardo. *Elections, Electoral Systems and Volatile Voters* (New York: Palgrave Macmillan, 2009), 5.

DEMOCRACY THROUGH THE AGES (pp. 6–11)

1. John V. A. Fine, *The Ancient Greeks: A Critical History* (Cambridge, MA: Belknap Press of Harvard University, 1985), 239.

2. Education Place, "The Roman Republic," http://www.eduplace.com/ss/socsci/ca/books/bkf3/reviews/pdfs/LS_6_13_02.pdf.

3. Fine, *The Ancient Greeks*, 381–90.

4. UK Parliament, "Birth of the English Parliament: Magna Carta (1215) to Henry IV (1399)," http://www.parliament.uk/about/living-heritage/evolutionofparliament/originsofparliament/birthofparliament/keydates/1215to1399.

5. Lee Stewart, "The Declaration of Rights," The Glorious Revolution, http://www.thegloriousrevolution.org/docs/declarationofrights.htm.

6. UK Parliament, "Birth of the English Parliament: Rise of the Commons," http://www.parliament.uk/about/living-heritage/evolutionofparliament/originsofparliament/birthofparliament/overview/riseofcommons.

7. The Papers of George Washington, "George Washington, Letter to Bryan Fairfax, July 20, 1774," http://gwpapers.virginia.edu/documents/revolution/letters/bfairfax2.html.

8. The History Guide, "The Origins of the French Revolution, Lectures on Modern European History," http://www.historyguide.org/intellect/lecture11a.html.

9. The Choices Program, "Egypt's Uprising," http://www.choices.edu/resources/twtn_egypt.php.

10. Peter Kenyon, "As Egypt Moves Toward Elections, Anxiety Grows," National Public Radio, May 17, 2011.

11. Jennifer Preston, "Movement Began with Outrage and a Facebook Page That Gave It an Outlet," *New York Times*, February 5, 2011, http://www.nytimes.com/2011/02/06/world/middleeast/06face.html?_r=1.

12. Jayme Poisson, "Google Marketing Manager Hero of Egypt's Uprising," *The Star*, February 8, 2011, http://www.thestar.com/news/world/article/934855–google-marketing-manager-hero-of-egypt-s-uprising.

13. John Guardiano, "Egypt's Internet Revolution Succeeds," Frum Forum, February 11, 2011, http://www.frumforum.com/egypts-internet-revolution-succeeds.

DEMOCRACY IN ACTION (pp. 12–17)

1. Nadim Audi, "Offering Slow, Small Changes, Morocco's King Stays in Power," *Pittsburgh Post-Gazette*, July 11, 2011, http://www.post-gazette.com/pg/11192/1159693-82-0.stm?cmpid=nationworld.xml#ixzz1UqCFuvUc.

2. Nicola McEwen, "The UK Constitution: Governing the UK," BBC News, September 1, 2003, http://news.bbc.co.uk/2/hi/programmes/bbc_parliament/2561719.stm.

3. Bartleby, "Respectfully Quoted: A Dictionary of Quotations," http://www.bartleby.com/73/991.html.

4. McEwen, "The UK Constitution."

5. "Gore: 'It Is Time for Me to Go,'" The Guardian, December 14, 2000, http://www.guardian.co.uk/world/2000/dec/14/uselections2000.usa14.

6. Voting for Judges, "Frequently Asked Questions," http://votingforjudges.org/11pri/faq.html;

7. Australian Politics, "The Westminster System," http://australianpolitics.com/key-terms/westminster-system.

8. Ibid.

9. UK Parliament, "Proportional Representation," http://www.parliament.uk/site-information/glossary/proportional-representation.

10. Robert Gerenge, "The Electoral System for South Sudan: Apportioning Immediate to Long-term Needs," Election Guide Digest, http://digest.electionguide.org/2011/05/11/electoral-system-for-south-sudan-apportioning-immediate-to-long-term-needs.

11. Manuel Alvarez-Rivera, "Election Resources on the Internet: The Republic of South Africa Electoral System," Election Resources, http://electionresources.org/za/system/.

12. Gerenge, "Electoral System for South Sudan."

13. Ibid.

14. "South Sudan Passes Interim Constitution Amid Concerns Over Presidential Powers," Sudan Tribune, July 7, 2011, http://www.sudantribune.com/South-Sudan-passes-interim,39457.

THE ROLE OF PARTIES (pp. 18–27)

1. International IDEA, "Political Parties, Participation and Representation," http://www.idea.int/parties/index.cfm.

2. Radio Free Europe, "Kremlin Opponents Lose Putin Slander Suit," February 14, 2011.

3. Richard Hofstadter, The Idea of a Party System (Berkeley: University of California Press, 1969), 9–16.

4. Encyclopedia Britannica, s.v. "Indian National Congress," http://www.britannica.com/EBchecked/topic/285841/Indian-National-Congress.

5. Encyclopedia Britannica, s.v. "Shas," http://www.britannica.com/EBchecked/topic/755711/Shas.

6. Erik Amfitheatof, "Soviet Union: One Party, One Vote," Time, March 12, 1984, http://www.time.com/time/magazine/article/0,9171,921597-2,00.html.

7. H. P. Wilmott et al., World War II (New York: DK Publishing, 2004), 17–19.

8. Peter Ford, "90 Years of China's Communist Party: From Secret Society to 'harmonious society,'" Christian Science Monitor, July 2, 2011, http://www.csmonitor.com/World/Asia-Pacific/2011/0702/90-years-of-China-s-Communist-Party-from-secret-society-to-harmonious-society.

9. Associated Press, "Three New Political Parties Register in Egypt," USA Today, June 14, 2011, http://www.usatoday.com/news/world/2011-06-14-new-political-parties-egypt_n.htm.

10. Yevgeny Bendersky, "Democracy in the Former Soviet Union, 1991–2004," Eurasianet, January 2, 2005, http://www.eurasianet.org/departments/insight/articles/pp010305.shtml.

11. RT.com, "Opposition Party Denied Registration for Accepting Dead Members," http://rt.com/politics/opposition-party-denied-registration.

12. Ace Project, "Registration Requirements for Parties."

13. Ace Project: Electoral Knowledge Network, "Registration Requirements for Parties," http://aceproject.org/epic-en/CDTable?question=PC001&set_language=en.

14. Ace Project: Electoral Knowledge Network, "Independent Candidates," http://aceproject.org/epic-en/CDTable?question=PC008&set_language=en.

15. Roger Biles, Encyclopedia of Chicago History, s.v. "Machine Politics," http://www.encyclopedia.chicagohistory.org/pages/774.html.

16. Derick W. Brinkerhoff and Arthur A. Goldsmith, "Clientelism, Patrimonialism and Democratic Governance: An Overview and Framework for Assessment and Programming," U.S. Agency for International Development, http://pdf.usaid.gov/pdf_docs/PNACR426.pdf.

17. International IDEA, "Political Parties, Participation and Representation," http://www.idea.int/parties/index.cfm.

18. Magdalene Sey, "Politicians Most Corrupt—TI," *The Ghanaian Journal*, March 4, 2011, http://www.theghanaianjournal.com/2011/03/04/politicians-most-corrupt-ti.

19. Joe Allbaugh, "'Can I Quit Now?' FEMA Chief Wrote as Katrina Raged," CNN.com, November 4, 2005, http://articles.cnn.com/2005-11-03/us/brown.fema.emails_1_international-arabian-horse-association-marty-bahamonde-e-mails?_s=PM:US.

20. International IDEA, "Code of Conduct for Political Parties: Campaigning in Democratic Elections," http://www.idea.int/publications/coc_campaigning/upload/polparties.pdf.

21. International IDEA, "Thai Political Parties Sign Up to a Code of Conduct Before July Elections," http://www.idea.int/asia_pacific/thailand-pp-code-conduct.cfm.

CAMPAIGNS (pp. 28–37)

1. Coco Masters, "Japan's Twitter-Free Election Campaign," *Time*, August 18, 2009, http://www.time.com/time/world/article/0,8599,1917137,00.html.

2. Yoree Koh, "Tweeting Election Day, A First in Japan," *Wall Street Journal*, September 14, 2010, http://blogs.wsj.com/japanrealtime/2010/09/14/tweeting-election-day-a-first-in-japan/.

3. Law Library of Congress, "Campaign Finance: Comparative Summary," http://www.loc.gov/law/help/campaign-finance/comparative-summary.php.

4. Kasie Hunt and Maggie Haberman, "Romney Fundraising to Begin in April," Politico, March 31, 2011, http://www.politico.com/blogs/bensmith/0311/Romney_fundraising_to_begin_in_April.html.

5. ACE Project: Electoral Knowledge Network, "Candidate Selection Within Political Parties," http://aceproject.org/ace-en/topics/pc/pcb/pcb02/pcb02a/onePage.

6. PBS, "*Campaign*: Film Description," http://www.pbs.org/pov/campaign/film_description.php.

7. World Movement for Democracy, "International Knowledge Network of Women in Politics," http://www.wmd.org/assemblies/fifth-assembly/reports/functional-networking/international-knowledge-network-women-politi.

8. International IDEA, "India: Reservation."

9. John Lloyd, "Out of the Ruins," *Financial Times*, July 7, 2006, http://cdd.stanford.edu/press/2006/ft-ruins.pdf.

10. Open Secrets, "Presidential Candidate Barack Obama," http://www.opensecrets.org/pres08/summary.php?id=n00009638.

11. James L. Martin, "Mother's Milk of Politics," *Washington Times*, December 7, 2008, http://www.washingtontimes.com/news/2008/dec/07/mothers-milk-of-politics.

12. BBC News, "Donor's Knighthood 'Undermines System,'" June 17, 2002, http://cdnedge.bbc.co.uk/1/hi/uk_politics/2045417.stm.

13. International Foundation for Electoral Systems, "Global Practices in Campaign Finance," November 23, 2009, http://www.ifes.org/Content/Publications/News-in-Brief/2009/Nov/Global-Practices-in-Campaign-Finance-an-Excerpt-from-IFES-New-Book.aspx.

14. Public Campaign, "Brief History of Fair Elections Victories," http://www.publicampaign.org/briefhistory.

15. Ace Project: Electoral Knowledge Network, "Public Funding of Parties," http://aceproject.org/epic-en/CDTable?question=PC012&set_language=en.

16. Magnus Öhman and Hani Zainulbhai, eds., *Political Finance Regulation: The Global Experience* (Washington, DC: International Foundation for Electoral Systems, 2009), 73.

17. Law Library of Congress, "Campaign Finance: Comparative Summary," http://www.loc.gov/law/help/campaign-finance/comparative-summary.php.

18. International Foundation for Electoral Systems, "Global Practices in Campaign Finance," http://www.ifes.org/Content/Publications/News-in-Brief/2009/Nov/Global-Practices-in-Campaign-Finance-an-Excerpt-from-IFES-New-Book.aspx.

19. CQ Rollcall, "Political Action Committees," http://corporate.cqrollcall.com/wmspage.cfm?parm1=233.

20. Supreme Court.gov, "Citizens United v. Federal Election Committee, 558 U.S. 08-205 (2010)," http://www.supremecourt.gov/opinions/09pdf/08-205.pdf.

21. Adam Liptak, "Justices, 5–4, Reject Corporate Spending Limit," New York Times, January 21, 2010, http://www.nytimes.com/2010/01/22/us/politics/22scotus.html.

22. International Foundation for Electoral Systems, "Dirty Money in Politics: How El Padrino's Contributions Affect Security in Latin America," http://216.65.11.186/Content/Videos/2011/How-El-Padrinos-Contributions-Affect-Security-in-Latin-America.aspx.

23. Liz Harper, "Colombia's Civil War: Revolutionary Armed Forces of Colombia (FARC)," Online NewsHour, http://www.cocaine.org/colombia/farc.html.

24. Michael Martinez, "Study: Colombian Rebels Were Willing to Kill for Venezuela's Chavez," CNN.com, May 10, 2011, http://articles.cnn.com/2011-05-10/world/venezuela.farc.documents_1_farc-leader-raul-reyes-colombian-rebels?_s=PM:WORLD.

25. BBC News, "Ehud Olmert: Corruption Allegations," May 3, 2010, http://news.bbc.co.uk/2/hi/middle_east/7035526.stm.

THE ROLE OF THE MEDIA IN VOTING AND ELECTIONS (pp. 38–41)

1. Chun-Fang Chian, "Sources of Media Bias," National Taiwan University, http://homepage.ntu.edu.tw/~chunfang/Bias.pdf.

2. Roy Greenslade, "Murdoch Has Too Much Political Influence, Say 60% in Poll," The Guardian, March 19, 2011, http://www.guardian.co.uk/media/greenslade/2011/mar/19/rupert-murdoch-polls.

3. Toby Helms and James Robinson, "Phone Hacking: Rupert Murdoch 'Urged Gordon Brown' to Halt Labour Attacks," The Guardian, April 9, 2011, http://www.guardian.co.uk/uk/2011/apr/09/phone-hacking-rupert-murdoch-gordon-brown.

4. Tony Dokoupil, "How Global Politics Got Starbucked," Newsweek, May 10, 2008, http://www.thedailybeast.com/newsweek/2008/05/10/how-global-politics-got-starbucked.html.

5. Christina Holtz-Bacha and Lynda Lee Kaid, "Political Advertising in International Comparison," Sage Publications, http://www.sagepub.com/upm-data/11717_Chapter1.pdf.

6. Law Library of Congress, "Campaign Finance: Germany," http://www.loc.gov/law/help/campaign-finance/germany.php.

7. FactCheck.org, "Republican-Funded Group Attacks Kerry's War Record," August 22, 2004, http://www.factcheck.org/article231.html.

8. MSNBC.com, "Bush Calls for Halt to Swift Boat Veterans' Ads," August 23, 2004, http://www.msnbc.msn.com/id/5797164/ns/politics/t/bush-calls-halt-swift-boat-veterans-ads/#.TkZ1LIJ15Sc.

9. Andrew Culf, "Demon Eyes Ad Wins Top Award," The Guardian, January 10, 1997, http://www.guardian.co.uk/politics/1997/jan/10/past.andrewculf.

10. Brendan O'Neill, "The Mumsnet Election: It's a Poisonous Divide," The First Post, April 13, 2010, http://www.thefirstpost.co.uk/62059,news-comment,news-politics,the-mumsnet-election-its-a-poisonous-divide-general-election-labour-conservatives.

11. Anjana Pasricha, "Nepal's Youth Turn to Social Media in Constitution Campaign," Voice of America, May 31, 2011, http://www.voanews.com/english/news/Nepals-Youth-Turn-to-Social-Media-in-Constitution-Campaign-122860749.html.

12. Ibid.

13. Jose Antonio Vargas, "Obama Raised Half a Billion Online," Washington Post, November 20, 2008, http://voices.washingtonpost.com/44/2008/11/obama-raised-half-a-billion-on.html.

14. Jennifer Aaker and Victoria Chang, "Obama and the Power of Social Media and Technology," The European Business Review, http://www.europeanbusinessreview.com/?p=1627.

VOTERS AND THE VOTING PROCESS (pp. 42–53)

1. Andrew Stengel, "Civic Literacy Test: Poll Tax Redux," The Huffington Post, November 21, 2007.

2. ACE Project: The Electoral Knowledge Network, "Overview of Voter Registration," http://aceproject.org/ace-en/topics/vr/vr10.

3. ProCon.org, "International Comparison of Felon Voting Laws," http://felonvoting.procon.org/view.resource.php?resourceID=000289.

4. ACE Project: The Electoral Knowledge Network, "Definition of Mental Illness in Electoral Law," http://aceproject.org/electoral-advice/archive/questions/replies/493785866.

5. "Saudi King Gives Women Right To Vote," National Public Radio, September 25, 2011, http://www.npr.org/2011/09/25/140784104/saudi-king-gives-women-right-to-vote?ft=1&f=1001

6. International IDEA, "Compulsory Voting," http://www.idea.int/vt/compulsory_voting.cfm.

7. Center for Voting and Democracy, "Voter Turnout," http://www.fairvote.org/voter-turnout.

8. International IDEA, "Voter Turnout for United Kingdom," http://www.idea.int/vt/country_view.cfm?CountryCode=GB.

9. Today's Zaman, "Dozens Detained Across Turkey for Attempted Election Fraud," June 12, 2011, http://www.todayszaman.com/news-247093-dozens-detained-across-turkey-for-attempted-election-fraud.html.

10. Ace Project: The Electoral Knowledge Network, "Legal Provisions to Prevent Fraud," http://aceproject.org/ace-en/topics/vr/vra/vra16.

11. John Hirst, Australia's Democracy: A Short History (Crow's Nest, Australia: Allen & Unwin, 2002), 50–51.

12. Bangkok Post, "Troubled Path to Election in Buri Ram," June 24, 2011, http://www.bangkokpost.com/breakingnews/243802/troubled-path-to-election-in-buri-ram.

13. Jason Burke, "Indian Government Tried to Buy Votes, Says WikiLeaks Cable," The Guardian, March 17, 2011, http://www.guardian.co.uk/world/2011/mar/17/india-usa.

14. Christopher Beam, "What's 'Street Money'?" Slate, October 23, 2008, http://www.slate.com/id/2202955/.

15. Election Commission of India, "About ECI," http://eci.nic.in/eci_main/about-eci/the_setup.asp.

16. United Nations, "Department of Political Affairs: Africa," http://www.un.org/wcm/content/site/undpa/main/activities_by_region/africa.

17. Zack Baddorf, "Burundi: Boycott Cedes Power To Ruling Party," All Africa, July 27, 2010, http://allafrica.com/stories/201007270004.html.

18. Vishal Agraharkar, Wendy Weiser, and Adam Skaggs, "The Cost of Voter ID Laws: What the Courts Say," Brennan Center for Justice, http://brennan.3cdn.net/2f0860fb73fd559359_zzm6bhnld.pdf.

19. Andrew Ellis, "The Use and Design of Recall Votes," International IDEA, http://www.idea.int/democracy/upload/use_and_design_of_recall_votes.pdf.

20. International IDEA, "When Citizens Can Recall Elected Officials," Direct Democracy: The International IDEA Handbook, http://www.idea.int/publications/direct_democracy/upload/direct_democracy_handbook_chapter5.pdf.

21. Jennifer L. McCoy, "The 2004 Venezuelan Recall Referendum," Taiwan Journal of Democracy 2, no. 1, http://www.tfd.org.tw/docs/dj0201/Jennifer%20L.%20McCoy.pdf.

22. Online NewsHour, "California in Context," October 8, 2003, http://www.pbs.org/newshour/bb/politics/july-dec03/recall_10-08.html.

23. League of Women Voters of Illinois, "Recall of the Governor: Proposed Amendment to the Illinois Constitution," http://www.lwvil.org/recall_quickfacts.pdf.

24. The History Place, "Presidential Impeachment Proceedings: Bill Clinton," http://www.historyplace.com/unitedstates/impeachments/clinton.htm.

25. Alissa J. Rubin and Carlotta Gall, "Widespread Fraud Seen in Latest Afghan Elections," New York Times, September 24, 2010, http://www.nytimes.com/2010/09/25/world/asia/25afghan.html.

FIND OUT MORE

Books

Carpentiere, Elizabeth Crooker, ed. *Elections: Voting Around the World* (Faces). Peterborough, N.H.: Cobblestone, 2008.

Delury, George E., and Neil Schlager, eds. *World Encyclopedia of Political Systems and Parties*. New York: Facts on File, 2006.

Downing, David. *Democracy* (Political and Economic Systems). Chicago: Heinemann Library, 2007.

Marzilli, Alan. *Election Reform* (Point–Counterpoint). New York: Chelsea House, 2011.

Scherer, Randy, ed. *Political Scandals* (At Issue). Detroit: Greenhaven, 2008.

Steele, Philip. *Vote* (Eyewitness). New York: Dorling Kindersley, 2008.

Websites

There are many news websites that cover voting and elections, including the following:

aceproject.org/ace-en
This site offers information on how elections are carried out around the world.

www.congress.org/about
This site gives voters information on many important issues in U.S. politics.

www.electionguide.org
This site shows news on international elections by country or type of election.

www.idea.int
This site offers facts on the election process for more than 100 nations.

www.usa.gov/Citizen/Topics/Voting.shtml
This site from the U.S. government tells voters how to contact elected officials and explains the voting process, with information on voting laws in each state.

Suggestions for further research

Find out which countries will be having national elections this year. Choose one and list the major parties running and what their candidates propose to do if elected. Are there any issues about possible corruption or fraud?

Learn more about the electoral system in your country. What form of government does it have? What is the minimum voting age? Is voting compulsory? What are the major parties, and which one currently controls the legislative branch?

INDEX